Greg Brown

a taste
of browns

Photography by

Mark Chew and **Sally-Ann Balharrie**

VIKING

The authors and publisher would like to thank the
following people for the loan of props for photography:
Andrew Gourlay, French Style, Melbourne (03 9510 5833);
Guy Matthews and Alicia Homes-Smith, Rivet Junior Industrial
Furniture (03 9530 2309);
Charlotte and Pierre Julien (03 9534 5813);
Zanny Twopeny, Pinmoney, Melbourne (03 9427 9436).

References

Elizabeth David, *An Omelette and a Glass of Wine* (Penguin,
Harmondsworth, 1990); Jane Grigson, *Good Things* (Penguin,
Harmondsworth, 1990); Colin Spencer and Claire Clifton (eds),
The Faber Book of Food (Faber & Faber, London, 1993);
Margaret Visser, *Much Depends on Dinner* (Penguin,
Harmondsworth, 1992); Penny Smith, *The Epicurean Diary of
Food for Thought 1990* (Allen & Unwin, Melbourne, 1990).

Viking
Penguin Books Australia Ltd
487 Maroondah Highway, PO Box 257
Ringwood, Victoria 3134, Australia
Penguin Books Ltd
Harmondsworth, Middlesex, England
Viking Penguin, A Division of Penguin Books USA Inc.
375 Hudson Street, New York, New York 10014, USA
Penguin Books Canada Limited
10 Alcorn Avenue, Toronto, Ontario, Canada M4V 3B2
Penguin Books (N.Z.) Ltd
182-190 Wairau Road, Auckland 10, New Zealand

First published by Penguin Books Australia Ltd 1995

10 9 8 7 6 5 4 3 2 1

Copyright © Greg Brown, Sally-Ann Balharrie
and Mark Chew, 1995

Printed and bound through Bookbuilders, Hong Kong

National Library of Australia
Cataloguing-in-Publication data

Brown, Greg. 1957- .
  A taste of browns.

  Includes index.
  ISBN 0 670 86444 7.

  1. Baking. 2. Bread. 3. Cake. 4. Pastry.
  I. Balharrie, Sally-Ann. II. Chew, Mark. III. Title.

641.71

C O N T E N T S

INTRODUCTION 1

B R E A D

SAN FRANCISCO SOUR DOUGH 18

WALNUT AND RAISIN STICKS 20

SOUR RYE BREAD 22

BAGUETTES 26

FLAT OLIVE BREAD 29

T A R T S

SMOKED SALMON QUICHE 36

SEASONAL FRUITELLA TART 38

MR ROUX'S LEMON TART 41

GOAT'S CHEESE TARTS 42

PASSIONFRUIT TART 46

C A K E S

LAMINGTONS 54

DOUBLE-BAKED CHOCOLATE CAKE 56

CARROT CAKE 58

CONCORDE 61

FLOURLESS CHOCOLATE MUFFINS 66

ORANGE AND POPPYSEED CAKE 68

PEACH CHARLOTTE 71

PATISSERIE

CROISSANTS **80**

CHEESE STICKS **83**

DOUGHNUTS **85**

PAIN AU CHOCOLAT **86**

SAVOURY BRIOCHES **88**

GOUGÈRE **91**

BISCOTTI GARIBALDI **93**

VANILLA SLICE **96**

CELEBRATIONS

HEART-SHAPED RASPBERRY CHARLOTTE **100**

CHOCOLATE AND RASPBERRY TARTLETTES (*petits fours*) **105**

ALMOND MACAROONS (*petits fours*) **106**

CHOCOLATE MACAROONS (*petits fours*) **106**

LEMON TARTLETTES (*petits fours*) **107**

COCONUT TUILES (*petits fours*) **109**

HOT CROSS BUNS **110**

PLUM PUDDING **115**

THE BASICS

CUSTARD **120**

RASPBERRY MOUSSE **121**

LEAVEN PASTRY **122**

SABLÉ PASTRY **123**

PUFF PASTRY **124**

SHEET SPONGE **125**

GÉNOISE SPONGE **126**

INDEX OF RECIPES **127**

To Merran

A woman who gives

everything and asks

for nothing

You want adventure? Become a chef.

A TASTE OF BROWNS is a small insight into the way I think about food. During the course of putting this book together I was continually struck, and humbled, by how excited and entranced my co-authors Sally-Ann Balharrie and Mark Chew were by my kitchen. Their reaction prompted me to recall why I had started cooking professionally in the first place: to share what I know, to evoke tastes and memories of home, and to play and experiment with food. ¶ Great food has the ability to recapture a memory, and, more importantly, create new ones. My grandmother, for instance, makes the most delicious chocolate cake, which I suspect comes out of a trusty Country Women's Association cookbook. She so loves and cares

for this humble cake, and puts her whole heart and soul into baking it, that you can almost taste her beating the butter and sugar and see her eyes watering as she checks the cake in the hot, steamy oven. I love that cake. ¶ Cooking, you see, is not just a process. It is about people, their lives and the changing seasons. The flour we use at the bakery, for example, comes from an old-fashioned mill that uses traditional European techniques. The flour they produce is beautifully creamy, and when you crush a handful of it, you can actually smell the wheat. That is the essence of good food – pure and uncontaminated origins and a great deal of care. Indeed, most of our recipes come out of three simple ingredients – flour,

h o n e s t y

butter and perspiration, surely, the true test of a loving cook! ¶ Good food is not the exclusive domain of restaurants, however. Nor is it necessarily complicated. The recipes collected here are some of my great favourites, from the simple, honest Carrot Cake to the elegant Lemon Tart by Mr Roux. Many are ideal for the family, and others, such as the flamboyant Concorde, will wow your dinner guests. These, I hope, are recipes you will share with your family and friends, be it in celebration or solace. ¶ The fostering and sharing of ideas and techniques is fundamental to anything that is worth doing. It is a philosophy I cling to, a legacy of the time I spent with Mr Roux at the Waterside Inn Buckinghamshire, UK. From

3

continued on page 7

It may be said that **perfection** only belongs to God, but my bakers and chefs believe they can visit it for three seconds every day and do it all again the next day.

Greg Brown

him I learnt that a fine restaurant is the sum of its parts and is all about perfection. ¶ The bakery had a humble start in the Browns restaurant kitchen, and from three people who worked too hard and long into the night, we now have seventy-four staff who keep halfway sane hours. The logistics of baking nearly 10,000 loaves of bread for weekends is the only thing that has changed. I get enormous pleasure from the hustle and bustle of my kitchens, and from seeing people **passion** work with their hands and cut a loaf of bread from a batch, poking and smelling it. ¶ I am immensely lucky to have bakers and pastry chefs who share my attitude to food, and indeed A TASTE OF BROWNS is as much a story of their development as it is mine. Together, our ambition is to achieve more than just a product on the shelf; what we want to do is create something that looks good, feels good, smells good and tastes good. It may be said that perfection only belongs to God, but my bakers and chefs believe that they can visit it for three seconds every day and do it all again the next day. ¶ It is my hope that you will be inspired to take the same journey and enjoy the delicious flavours as you go through the recipes and Sally-Ann and Mark's beautiful photographs. Good cooking, after all, is not about involved techniques and gizmos, it is about love and enjoyment. ¶ Happy cooking, eating and sharing. ¶ Greg Brown ¶

d e d i c a t i o n

WHILE THANKS go to all my staff for making things happen again and again, special mention is due to Ben Reed, who, at the tender age of 24, is now our Production Manager. He has been with us for five years, having embarked on his working career as a jockey. Unfortunately, he continued to grow and ended up behind a stove in a country hotel. He then joined Browns restaurant, where he worked his way up through the kitchen. Together we have become addicts to our adrenaline as we work through the night to prepare the bakery for the following day. ¶ Phillip Mutton, our head Pastry Chef, is the most caring, gentle pastry chef with whom I have ever worked. ¶ He approaches his craft with the

skill and aplomb of a surgeon. ¶ Darren Belfield, our Head Baker, cares for his doughs as a new mother would her child. ¶ My brother Chris, who manages the company, has brought a new sense of controlled order to the team at Browns – so far I have escaped his influence. ¶ Merran Brown, arguably the better half of Browns, shared the original dream and made it happen and now maintains it. Merran gave up her career in Sociology to become a chef's widow, and our shops are a testament to her impeccable taste. A regal mother, Browns would be impoverished without her. ¶ To Phil Mutton. ¶ To my friends at Viking. ¶ To Caroline Pizzey. ¶ And Craig McVean for his tireless support. ¶

Cooking is an art;

it demands hard
and sometimes
distasteful work,
but on the whole
it is the creative
side that prevails.

Constance Spry

bread

A good, fresh, and affordable **piece of bread** should be in everyone's hands.

Greg Brown

San Francisco Sour Dough

FERMENT

175 ml water

125 g sultanas,

roughly chopped

STARTER

500 g bakers' flour

725 ml water

DOUGH

2 kg bakers' flour

1–2 litres water

3 tablespoons salt

• For the Ferment, combine the water and sultanas and allow to sit for a week.

• For the Starter, mix 75 ml of the ferment with the flour and water in a 5-litre bucket. Allow to rise for 24 hours.

• For the Dough, put 500 g of the starter, the flour and 500 ml of the water in a large mixing bowl with a dough hook. (After its initial use, the starter needs to be fed 1 cup each of flour and water daily to keep it alive and the flavour mild.) Mix slowly, carefully adding more water by pouring it down the sides of the bowl and underneath the ball of dough. When the dough is wet and sticky, add the salt and mix slowly for 12 minutes.

• Rest the dough, covered with a tea towel, in a warm place for 3 hours.

• Divide into 3 cobs (about 750 g each). Rest for 30 minutes, covered with a tea towel dusted with flour, in a mould to help it hold its shape. Leave in a warm place to rise for 9-14 hours.

• Preheat the oven to 200°C. Score each cob with a razor blade and bake for 50–60 minutes. Remove from the oven and allow to cool on a wire rack.

Makes 3

Walnut and Raisin Sticks

350g bakers' flour

1/4 cup wholemeal

plain flour

1/4 cup bran

1 heaped tablespoon sugar

330ml water

12g (1 sachet) dry yeast

1 tablespoon salt

100g walnuts

100g raisins

• Put the flours, bran and sugar into a mixing bowl with a dough hook.

• Combine the water and yeast and add to the flour. Mix with a dough hook for 8 minutes.

• Add the salt, walnuts and raisins and mix for a further 2 minutes.

• Remove the dough from the bowl and cut into two equal portions and place in two 500g bread tins. Cover with a tea towel and allow to prove in a warm place for 40 minutes.

• Preheat the oven to 180°C and bake for 20 minutes. Leave to cool in the bread tins.

• Serve with cheese and fruit. Walnut and Raisin Sticks freeze well if wrapped tightly in freezer bags.

Note: If you have pencil moulds, cut the dough into four 250g pieces and put into the oiled moulds. Allow to prove for 30–40 minutes and bake for 20 minutes.

Makes 2

Sour Rye Bread

1 kg bakers' flour

2 tablespoons salt

1/2 teaspoon gluten

6 g (1/2 sachet) dry yeast

750 ml water

STARTER

500 g rye flour

500 ml water

375 ml wheat beer

• To make the Starter, mix the rye flour, water and beer in a 5-litre bucket. Allow to develop for 2–4 days before using, feeding it daily with 1 cup each of rye flour and water.

• In a large bowl, mix all the dry ingredients for 2 minutes. Add 300 g of the starter and the water and mix for a further 7 minutes or until the dough has developed. Rest the dough for at least 10 minutes.

• Form two round cobs of 750 g each and use the remaining dough to make small rolls. Prove, covered with a tea towel, in a warm place for 40 minutes.

• Preheat the oven to 220°C. Sprinkle the loaves and rolls with flour and cut a cross into the top of each cob using a razor blade. Bake the bread for 40 minutes. The rolls will take 15 minutes.

Makes 2 cobs and a few small rolls

This recipe requires attention and is more challenging than the others.

Flat Olive Bread

250 g bakers' flour

6 g (¹/₂ sachet) dry yeast

³/₄ tablespoon salt

150 ml water

3 tablespoons olive oil

1 heaped tablespoon dried
mixed herbs

12 black olives, cut in
half and stoned

• Combine the flour and yeast in a mixing bowl with a dough hook.

• Dissolve half the salt in the water and then add the olive oil, reserving 2 teaspoons for later use.

• Pour the liquid into the flour and yeast. Mix with a dough hook until the dough clears the side of the bowl and makes popping and squeaking sounds.

• Remove the dough from the bowl and form two equal portions (about 250 g each). Roll out to 5 mm thick and set aside on a lightly oiled tray. Prove, covered with a tea towel, in a warm place for 30 minutes or until doubled in size.

• Preheat the oven to 220°C. With the tips of your fingers make fairly deep indentations on the surface of each loaf. Lightly brush with the reserved olive oil, sprinkle over the herbs and the remaining salt, and push the olive halves into the dough.

• Bake for about 25 minutes but do not allow to colour. Cool on a wire rack.

Makes 2

The flat olive bread
is left to prove, then the
tops are brushed with
olive oil. Herbs are
sprinkled over and
olives pressed into the
dough before
baking.

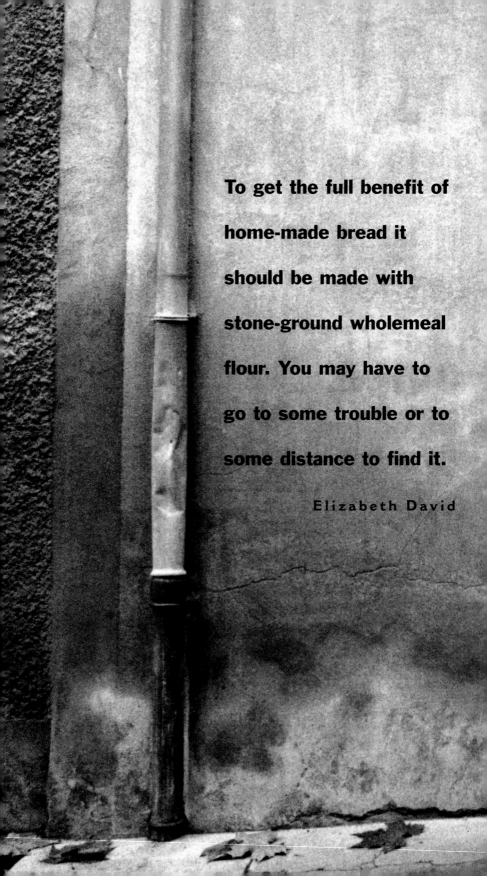

To get the full benefit of home-made bread it should be made with stone-ground wholemeal flour. You may have to go to some trouble or to some distance to find it.

Elizabeth David

tarts

Smoked Salmon Quiche

150 g tasty cheese, grated

300 g smoked salmon

350 ml milk

4 eggs

pinch of salt

5 sundried tomatoes, sliced

sprigs of dill

PASTRY

250 g bakers' flour

250 g plain flour

3/4 tablespoon salt

250 g unsalted butter, softened

1 egg

100 ml water

• To make the Pastry, put the dry ingredients into a mixing bowl with a dough hook. Add the butter in pieces and mix thoroughly. Add the egg and water and mix again. The dough is ready when it comes cleanly away from the sides of the bowl.

• On a lightly floured surface, roll out the pastry to 5 mm thickness.

• Butter a 30 cm x 3 cm quiche tin and line with the pastry. Refrigerate for 1 hour. Line the pastry case with foil and fill with pastry weights or beans. Bake blind at 180°C for 15–20 minutes. Allow to cool.

• Sprinkle the cheese over the bottom of the pastry case and add the salmon. Whisk the milk, eggs and salt together, and carefully pour over the salmon. Bake at 180°C for 25–30 minutes until slightly coloured.

• To serve, put the tomatoes in the centre of the quiche and scatter over the sprigs of dill.

Serves 10–12

Seasonal Fruitella Tart

300 g Sablé Pastry

(see page 123)

20 g butter

150 ml thickened cream

10 ml pear liqueur

1–2 mixed punnets

(350 g) seasonal fruit

(e.g. berries, red and

white currants, cherries)

5 mint leaves

50 g icing sugar

2 hours until it ceases to give out moisture.

• Fill the cooled pastry case with the cream and decorate with the fruit and mint leaves.

Serves 8–10

• Preheat the oven to 180°C.

• Roll the pastry out to 5 mm thickness and butter a 20 cm x 2 cm flan tin. Line the tin with pastry and bake for 15–20 minutes. Allow to cool.

• Whisk the cream with the pear liqueur until the mixture falls back on itself in a 'ribbon' when the whisk is lifted from the bowl.

• Transfer the mixture to a fine sieve and refrigerate, suspended over a bowl for

Mr Roux's Lemon Tart

4 lemons

9 eggs

375 g sugar

300 ml cream

650 g Sablé Pastry

(see page 123)

50 g icing sugar

• Finely grate the lemons, and then juice them.

• Break the eggs into a large bowl and add the sugar and mix well until light and frothy. Mix in the lemon juice and zest and the cream and refrigerate for up to 24 hours. (The mix is best prepared a day before it is required.)

• Preheat the oven to 180°C.

• Roll the pastry out to 5 mm thickness and butter a 20 cm x 5 cm flan tin. Line the tin with the pastry and then line the pastry with foil. Fill with pastry weights or beans and bake blind for 20 minutes or until the pastry is golden brown in colour. Allow to cool.

• Pour the lemon mixture into the cooled pastry case, leaving a 3–5 mm space from top and bake at 180°C for 1 hour or until set. The tart should not soufflé or have a domed top, and should be just set when shaken.

• Leave the tart to cool for at least 4 hours before removing the ring. Dust with icing sugar before serving.

Serves 10–12

Goat's Cheese Tarts

PASTRY

300 g plain flour

200 g unsalted butter,

    softened

120 ml water

a pinch of salt

FILLING

185 g goat's cheese

150 g ricotta

110 g mozzarella, grated

75 ml crème fraîche

1 heaped tablespoon

    freshly grated parmesan

pinch of salt

50 niçoise olives, pitted

• To make the Pastry, put the flour, butter, water and salt into a mixing bowl with a paddle (not a balloon whisk) and mix until well incorpo-rated. (If you don't have a mixer with a paddle, work the mixture on a lightly floured surface with the palms of your hands.)

• Wrap the pastry in plastic and refrigerate for 24 hours.

• Allow the pastry to come to room temperature. Divide the pastry into 60 g portions and roll each into 10 rounds about 3 mm thick. Roll out the remaining pastry and cut strips 4 mm wide x 2 mm thick. Rim each pastry round with a pastry strip that is laid flat on the round, ensuring that the outer edges meet. Crimp the edges slightly for a decorative finish.

• Preheat the oven to 180°C. In a mixing bowl with a paddle, mix all the Filling ingredients at once on a low speed.

• Fill each tart with the cheese mixture and decorate with the olives. Bake for 15–20 minutes. Serve immediately.

Makes 10

A brood of hens

A clutch of eggs

A sheaf of wheat

An aroma of

bakers

A range of ovens...

A loaf of **bread.**

James Lipton

Passionfruit Tart

16 passionfruit

4 eggs

180 g sugar

150 ml cream

650 g Sablé Pastry (see
page 123)

50 g icing sugar

• To obtain 150 ml passion-fruit juice, process the pulp in a blender for 5 seconds and strain the liquid.

• Break the eggs into a bowl and add the sugar. Whisk well, then add the passion-fruit juice and cream. Strain the mixture and refrigerate. (The mixture is best prepared a day before it is required.)

• Preheat the oven to 180°C. Roll the pastry out to 5 mm thickness and butter a 23 cm x 2 cm flan tin. Line the tin with pastry, rolling a lip over the sides, and line the pastry with foil. Fill with pastry weights or beans and bake blind for 20 minutes or until the pastry is golden brown. Allow to cool. Reduce the oven temperature to 170°C.

• Pour the passionfruit mixture into the cooled pastry case. Bake for 30 minutes or until the mixture is just set when shaken. Be very careful not to let the top soufflé or form a dome.

• Leave the tart to cool for at least 2 hours before removing the ring. Dust with icing sugar before serving.

Serves 10–12

A patisserie chef adding the finishing touches to a tartlette

cak

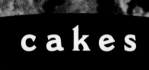

cakes

es

chocolate *n. 1.* a food preparation made from roasted ground cacao seeds, usually sweetened and flavoured. *2.* a drink or sweetmeat made from this. [C17: from Spanish, from Aztec *xocolatl*, from *xococ* sour, bitter + *atl* water]

Collins

Lamingtons

1 quantity Génoise Sponge

(see page 126)

300 g dark cooking

  chocolate

100 g copha

50 ml peanut oil

200 g coconut

- Preheat the oven to 180°C.
- To make lamingtons, prepare the sponge mixture as in the recipe. Bake in a lined 25 cm square cake tin for 30 minutes.
- Cut the cooled cake into 20 squares.
- Melt the chocolate with the copha in a double boiler and pour in the oil.
- Using a skewer or a fork, dip each piece of cake in the chocolate mixture and then roll it in the coconut.
- Leave the lamingtons to set on a wire rack.

Makes 20

Double-baked Chocolate Cake

330g dark chocolate

2 tablespoons
unsalted butter

4 eggs

12 egg whites

1 dessertspoon castor
sugar

3 level teaspoons
powdered gelatine

TO DECORATE

40g dark chocolate

40g white chocolate

• Preheat the oven to 180°C.

• Melt the chocolate and butter in a bowl over boiling water (or leave the bowl in a warm place) and stir in the egg yolks.

• In a separate bowl, beat the egg whites until light and fluffy, and add the sugar. Beat a further minute to form a meringue.

• Spoon a quarter of the meringue into the chocolate mixture, then fold the mixture back into the remaining meringue.

• Using a piping bag, half-fill a 23 cm x 2.5 cm cake ring and bake for 20 minutes. Allow to cool in the pan.

• Dissolve the gelatine in 2 tablespoons of warm water and fold into the remaining unbaked mixture. Spoon the mixture onto the cooled cake and level off with a spatula. Freeze until required and allow to come to room temperature before serving.

• To decorate the cake, melt the two chocolates separately and spoon into two paper piping cones. Decorate by criss-crossing the top of the cake with dark chocolate first, then with white chocolate in the opposite direction.

Serves 10–12

Carrot Cake

450 g sugar

5 eggs

230 g wholemeal flour

120 g plain flour

a pinch of cinnamon

1 dessertspoon baking
  powder

250 ml vegetable oil

440 g carrots, grated

1/2 cup walnuts, chopped
  roughly

TOPPING

125 g cream cheese

125 g unsalted butter,
  softened

100 g icing sugar

extra walnuts to decorate

• Preheat the oven to 180°C.

• Beat the sugar and eggs
until pale and sift the dry
ingredients into the bowl.
Add the oil, carrot and
walnuts and mix until
combined. Do not overmix

or the mixture will lose
too much volume.

• Butter two 21 cm x 7.5 cm
bread tins and line with baking paper. Divide the mixture
between the tins and bake
for 40 minutes or until the
cakes spring back when
touched. Allow to cool
in the tins.

• To make the Topping, beat
the cream cheese, butter and
icing sugar in a mixing bowl
with a paddle until light.

• Turn each cake upside
down and cover the top
(bottom) with topping. Make
a pattern in the topping with
a spatula and decorate with
the extra walnut meat.

Makes 2 cakes

Concorde

MERINGUE

150 g icing sugar

2 tablespoons cocoa

5 egg whites

150 g castor sugar

GANACHE

160 g dark chocolate

100 g unsalted butter

4 eggs, separated

2 tablespoons
  castor sugar

• Preheat the oven to 160°C.

• Sift the icing sugar and cocoa into a bowl. Beat the egg whites until stiff peaks form and, still mixing, add the castor sugar to make a firm meringue. Fold the icing sugar and cocoa through the meringue.

• Line a tray with baking paper.

• Using a piping bag with a plain medium-sized nozzle, pipe 12 disks 6 cm in diameter, and long lines (cigarettes) on a tray lined with baking paper. (Alternatively, make 1 large cake by piping 3 oval disks 22 cm x 14 cm instead of the 6 smaller ones.)

• Bake the meringue for 60 minutes. Turn off the heat and leave the meringue in the oven overnight.

• To make the Ganache, melt the chocolate and butter in a bowl over a saucepan of boiling water. Remove the saucepan from the heat and stir in 3 egg yolks. In another bowl, beat 4 egg whites until soft peaks form and mix in the castor sugar. Fold the beaten egg whites through the melted chocolate. Keep the ganache warm (or refrigerate and allow to come to room temperature before using).

• To assemble, spread   ➤

the ganache with a spatula on 6 of the disks and top with the remaining disks. Gently press the disks together, and smear ganache over the tops and sides. Gently break the meringue sticks into short pieces and stick them to the ganache so that they form a 'spiky' covering.

• Allow the concordes to sit in a refrigerator to firm up before serving. This can take up to 2 hours.

Serves 6

The ultimate indulgence – piped chocolate ganache swirls on chocolate cake

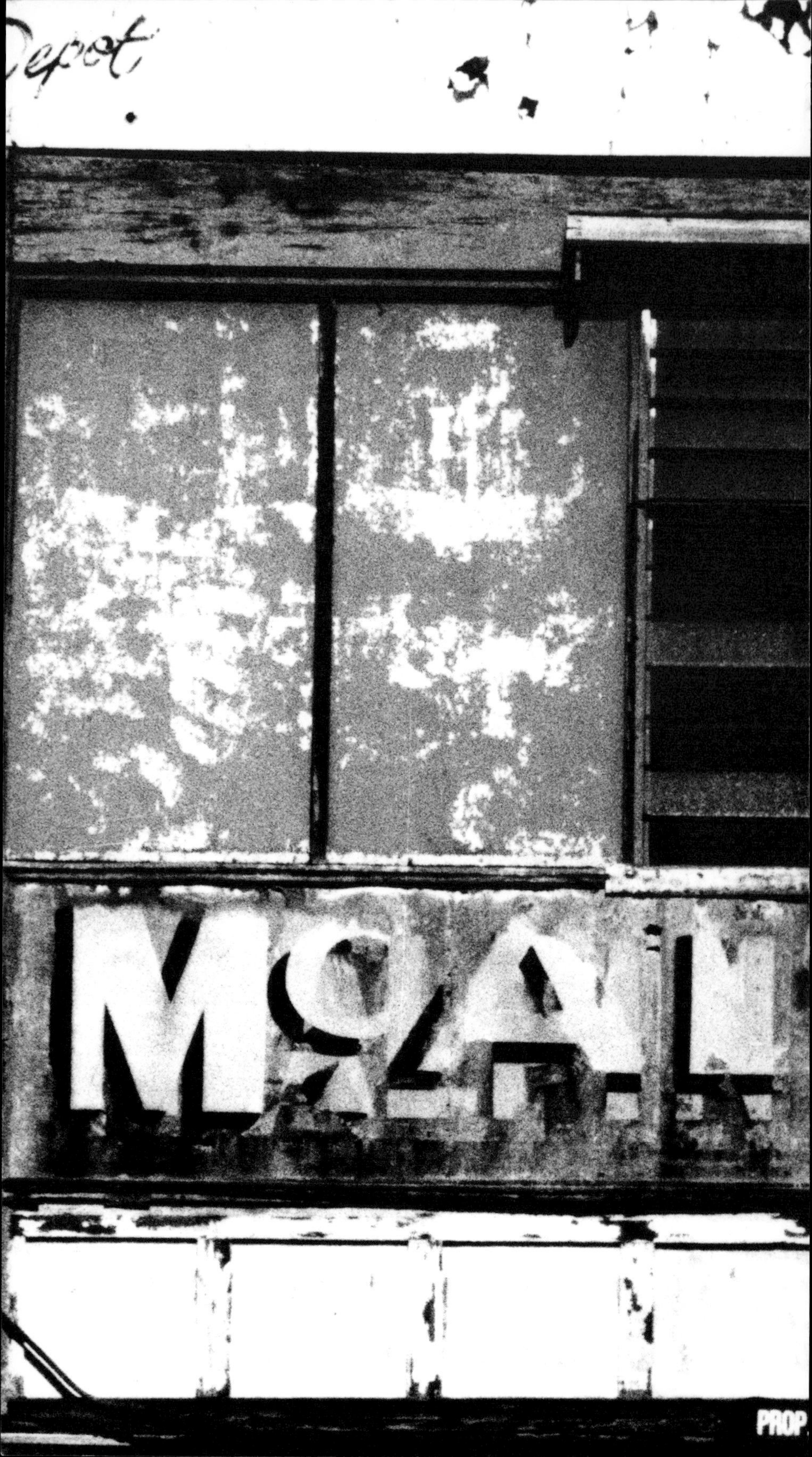

Depot
McAL
PROP.

Flourless Chocolate Muffins

600 g dark chocolate

500 g butter

12 eggs, separated

350 g sugar

240 g almond meal

1 teaspoon instant coffee

1 teaspoon cognac

150 g sugar

• Preheat the oven to 170°C. Grease petit pans or line and grease a 25 cm cake tin.

• Melt the chocolate and butter in a double boiler. Stir in the egg yolks, sugar and almond meal until well incorporated. Add the coffee and cognac. Allow the mixture to cool to room temperature.

• Whisk the egg whites until stiff peaks form and add in the sugar. Fold the meringue gently into the chocolate mixture.

• Fill a piping bag with a plain nozzle and pipe into the petit pans or pour into the prepared cake tin.

• If using petit pans, bake for 35 minutes. The larger chocolate cake will take around 50 minutes or until a skewer stuck in the middle comes out clean.

Makes 20 muffins or

1 large cake

Orange and Poppyseed Cake

6 eggs

440 g sugar

1 teaspoon salt

rind of 1 1/2 oranges,
  finely chopped

185 ml cream

340 g plain flour

1 teaspoon baking powder

1 dessertspoon
  poppyseeds

125 g unsalted butter,
  melted

50 g icing sugar (optional)

• Preheat the oven to 180°C.

• In a large bowl, whisk the eggs, sugar, salt, orange rind and cream for 5 minutes until light and fluffy.

• Sift in the flour and the baking powder and fold in the poppyseeds, followed by the butter.

• Butter two 21 cm x 7.5 cm bread tins and line with baking paper. Divide the mixture between the tins and bake for 40 minutes or until the cakes spring back when touched. Allow to cool in the tins.

• For a decorative finish, place a ruler lengthwise along the centre of each cake and dust with icing sugar.

Note: This cake is suitable for freezing.

Makes 2 cakes

Peach Charlotte

350 ml peach purée

70 ml peach juice

6 egg yolks

50 ml peach tree liqueur

7 teaspoons powdered

  gelatine

200 ml cream,

  semi-whipped

1 quantity Sheet Sponge

  (see page 125)

1 quantity Génoise Sponge

  (see page 126)

peach segments to

  decorate

MERINGUE

50 ml water

175 g sugar

3 egg whites

PUNCH

250 ml water

250 g sugar

25 ml peach tree liqueur

• Line a 18 cm x 6 cm cake
tin with baking paper.

• To make the Meringue, put
the water and sugar into a
saucepan and bring to the
boil.

• When the mixture is at
118°C (use a sugar ther-
mometer) start whipping the
egg whites in a mixer.

• When the sugar syrup
reaches 121°C, pour it slowly
down the edges of the bowl
into the whites. Keep whipping until the meringue has
cooled.

• To make a mousse, mix the
purée, juice and egg yolks
together in a double boiler
and cook until the mixture
coats the back of a spoon.

• Strain and add the gelatine.
Stir until the gelatine has
dissolved and cool over ice.
When cool, fold in the
meringue and then the
whipped cream.

• To make the Punch, bring
the sugar and water to ➤

the boil. Allow to cool and
add the peach liqueur.

• To assemble, cut 1 slice of
Sheet Sponge and line the
inside walls of the cake tin.

• Cut out 2 slices of the
Génoise Sponge about 1 cm
thick and slightly smaller
than the cake ring. Place one
of the slices in the bottom of
the cake ring and moisten
with punch.

• Pour the mousse to about
halfway up the ring, place
the other slice of sponge on
top and moisten with the
remaining punch.

• Fill the ring to the top with
the remaining mousse and
refrigerate.

• To serve, unmould the cake
and fan peach slices around
the top of the charlotte.

• Serve with Peach Sauce
(see page 120) if desired.

Serves 8–10

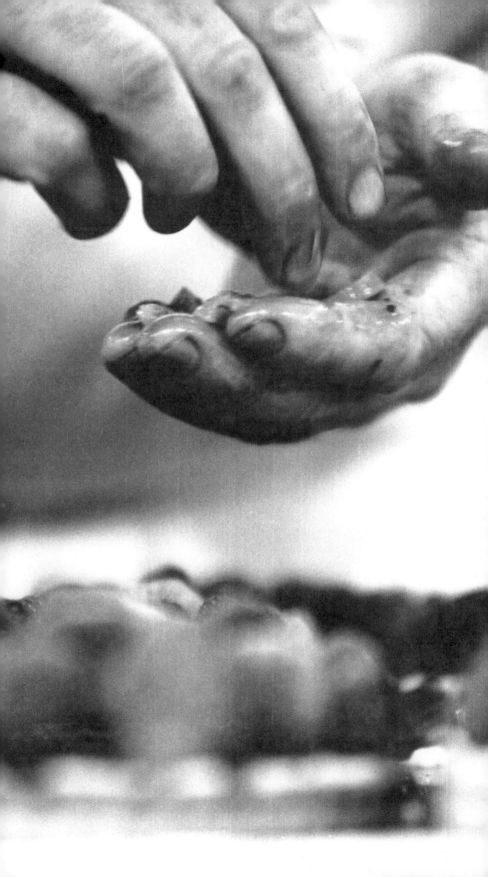

Coffee **glides** down

into one's stomach

and sets everything

in motion.

Balzac

paper

t

patisserie

s

s

i

e

That is the case now;

pastry-cooks are far

busier on **Sundays** and

holidays than at any

other times.

Louis-Sébastien Mercier,

The Picture of Paris, 1929

Croissants

1 quantity Leaven Pastry

(see page 122)

1 egg

pinch of salt

• Roll the dough out on a lightly floured surface to a thickness of 3 mm and cut the dough lengthwise into 18 cm wide strips. Cut this strip of pastry into triangles 14 cm wide at the base. Starting at the base, roll each triangle towards you using your open hand, being careful not to do this loosely as this will directly affect the end result. You may need to stretch the triangles through the middle slightly to attain four steps (rolls) in your croissants.

• Put the croissants on trays lined with baking paper and set aside to prove in a warm place for 1½ hours. The croissants should double in size, and when touched should spring back nicely without leaving impressions. Whisk together the egg and salt and lightly brush the tops of the croissants.

• Preheat the oven to 180°C. Bake for about 13 minutes or until golden brown on top, and lighter on the sides and at the same time crisp and flaky. Transfer the croissants onto a wire rack immediately after baking.

• Croissants are best served within 20 minutes after baking. However, they are still excellent reheated up to 6 hours after the initial bake and can be frozen for up to 2 weeks. To reheat, put the frozen croissants into a hot oven (250°C) for 5 minutes.

Makes 14

Doughnuts

440 g bakers' flour

pinch of salt

3 tablespoons sugar

70 ml water

12 g (1 sachet) dry yeast

5 eggs

220 g unsalted butter,
  softened

vegetable oil for frying

raspberry jam

castor sugar for coating

• Put the flour into a large mixing bowl with a dough hook. In a smaller bowl, combine the salt, sugar and 2 tablespoons of the water. Mix the liquid into the flour with the hook going slowly.

• Dissolve the yeast in the remaining water and add to the bowl with the dough hook mixing slowly. Add the eggs and mix until the dough clears the sides of the bowl. Add the butter in pieces and keep mixing until the dough is smooth.

• With lightly floured hands form the dough into 14 little balls. Set aside to prove uncovered in a warm place or until doubled in size.

• Pour the oil into a saucepan or deep-fryer to a depth of 10 cm. Heat to 175°C or until a little dough dropped into the oil floats to the surface and browns.

• Fry the doughnuts in batches, being careful not to crowd them, until golden brown (about 10 minutes). Remove the puffed, golden doughnuts to a wire rack to drain away any excess oil.

• With a piping bag, pipe a little raspberry jam into the middle of each doughnut while warm. Roll the filled doughnuts in castor sugar and allow to cool.

Makes 14

Pain au Chocolat

1 quantity Leaven Pastry
(see page 122)
280 g dark chocolate,
preferably in batons
1 egg
a pinch of salt

• To make Pain au Chocolat, roll out the pastry as for Croissants (see page 80). Cut into 100 mm x 120 mm rectangles.

• With the long side facing you, place one or two squares of chocolate on the top edge. Fold the dough over to enclose the chocolate and make a flattish cylindrical shape. Repeat this process with the remaining pastry.

• Place the pastries seam-side down on a tray lined with baking paper and set aside to prove in a warm place for 90 minutes or until doubled in size.

• Preheat the oven to 180°C.

Mix together the egg and salt and brush over the pastries. Bake for about 15 minutes or until golden brown on top, lighter on the sides and crisp and flaky. Transfer to a wire rack immediately.

• Best served within 20 minutes after baking, Pain au Chocolat can be reheated successfully up to 6 hours after the initial bake.

Makes 14

Savoury Brioches

220 g bakers' flour

a pinch of salt

2 tablespoons sugar

35 ml water

6 g (1/2 sachet) dry yeast

3 eggs

110 g unsalted butter,
softened

TOPPING

1 onion, sliced

120 g pumpkin, diced

1/2 red capsicum, diced

1/2 green capsicum, diced

100 g tasty cheese,
grated

8 broccoli florets

5 cherry tomatoes, halved

• For the Topping, glaze the onion in a little butter and blanch or steam the pumpkin, capsicum and broccoli. Set aside.

• Put the flour in a large mixing bowl with a dough hook. In a smaller bowl, combine the salt, sugar, yeast and water. Mix the liquid into the flour with the dough hook on a slow speed. Add the eggs and continue mixing until the dough clears the sides of the bowl. Add the butter in pieces and keep mixing until the dough is smooth.

• Remove the dough from the bowl with lightly floured hands and divide in two. Roll out to rounds of 5 mm thickness.

• Sprinkle the cheese over the dough, add the onions and decorate with the remaining vegetables. Set aside to prove, uncovered, in a warm place for about 40 minutes.

• Preheat the oven to 180°C. Bake the brioches for about 20 minutes or until golden.

Makes 2

Gougère

150 ml water

85 g unsalted butter

a pinch of salt

pinch of cayenne pepper

170 g strong flour

2 eggs, lightly beaten

85 g tasty cheese, grated

85 g Gruyère cheese,
grated

• Preheat the oven to 200°C.

• Put the water, butter, salt and cayenne pepper in a saucepan and bring to the boil. Add the flour and cook for 2–4 minutes, stirring continuously until the mixture coats the back of a spoon.

• Remove the saucepan from the heat and keep stirring to cool down the mixture. Stir in the eggs with a wooden spoon until incorporated, then fold in the tasty cheese.

• Line a tray with baking paper and spoon the mixture into a piping bag without a nozzle. Pipe 8 coiled shapes (or 16 for hors d'oeuvres) that start wide at the base and finish nice and high. Sprinkle over the Gruyère cheese.

• Bake for 20 minutes or until the outside is golden brown and the centre firm but moist.

• Serve hot from the oven or allow to cool on a wire rack.

Makes 8–16

Biscotti Garibaldi

50 g sugar

50 ml water

2 eggs

400 g sultanas

440 g Sablé Pastry

(see page 123)

• Over a low heat, melt the sugar until it caramelises. Deglaze with water and allow to cool.

• When the mixture is cool, whisk in the eggs.

• Roll out the Sablé Pastry into 2 rectangles measuring 30 cm x 20 cm.

• Brush the first sheet of pastry with the egg mixture and sprinkle over the sultanas. Roll them gently into the dough.

• Place the second layer of pastry on top and brush with the remaining egg mixture.

• Using a fork, comb the top of the pastry into a wave pattern. Wrap the pastry in plastic and refrigerate.

• When the pastry is firm enough to handle, cut into 7 cm x 2.5 cm rectangles. Bake for about 15 minutes at 180°C.

• Cool on a wire rack. Store in an airtight container.

Makes 40

There is a tendency, also,

to associate very dark

foods, such as coffee,

chocolate, truffles, caviar,

and *cèpes*, as well as plum

cake, with excitement and

luxury. We feel obscurely

that such **strange dark stuff**

must be meaningful and

ancient.

Margaret Visser

Vanilla Slice

**1 quantity Puff Pastry
(see page 124)**

1 1/2 cups icing sugar

2 tablespoons milk

**1/2 teaspoon vanilla
essence**

**1 1/2 teaspoon copha,
melted**

PASTRY CREAM

500 ml milk

1 vanilla pod, split

125 g sugar

6 egg yolks

3 tablespoons flour

**1 tablespoon custard
powder**

• For the Pastry Cream, simmer the milk with the vanilla pod. Place the sugar and egg yolks in a bowl and whisk until creamy. Fold in the flour and custard powder. Remove the pod and pour the milk into the yolk mixture, stirring continuously.

• Pour the mixture back into the saucepan and cook over a gentle heat until it coats the back of the spoon. Remove from the heat. Cover and refrigerate until ready to use.

• Preheat the oven to 175°C. Roll out the pastry to a 40 cm x 20 cm rectangle. Place between 2 baking trays with a 1 kg weight on top and bake for 15 minutes. Cut into 3 sheets measuring 13 cm x 20 cm.

• Spread the cream on one piece of pastry, place the next piece on top and spread with the remaining cream. Place the next piece of pastry on top and allow to set.

• For the icing, sift the icing sugar into a bowl. Add the milk, vanilla and copha. Spread onto the pastry and swirl over with melted chocolate, if desired.

Serves 6

celebration

Heart-shaped Raspberry Charlotte

50 g sugar

50 ml water

50 ml kirsch (optional)

1 quantity Sheet Sponge
   (see page 125)

1 quantity Raspberry
   Mousse (see page 121)

300 g fresh raspberries

100 g apricot jam

sprig of mint (optional)

• Put the sugar and water into a saucepan and bring to the boil. Remove from the heat and allow to cool. Stir in the kirsch, if desired, and set aside.

• To assemble the cake, cut 2 strips (32 cm x 3 cm) from the sponge and line the inside walls of a 64 cm x 3.5 cm heart-shaped tin. Using the point of a knife, cut out a piece of sponge slightly smaller than but the same shape as the tin and line the bottom. Moisten the form with a little of the cooled sugar syrup and scatter the raspberries over the sponge. Spoon the mousse into the tin and level it off. Refrigerate until set (about 8 hours).

• To serve, unmould the cake and decorate with the remaining raspberries. Warm the apricot jam and glaze the berries. Garnish the finished cake with a sprig of mint if you like.

Serves 8

Blackcurrants,

redcurrants,

raspberry tart,

tell me

the name

of your

sweetheart.

Skipping Rhyme

Chocolate and Raspberry Tartlettes

**150 g Sablé Pastry
(see page 123)
100 ml cream
100 g dark chocolate
1 dessertspoon unsalted
butter
1 punnet raspberries**

• Preheat the oven to 180°C.

• Roll out the pastry on a lightly floured surface to 3 mm thickness. Using a pastry cutter or knife, cut 20 rounds slightly larger than the petit four moulds (25 mm–30 mm). Lightly smear the moulds with butter and line with pastry. Trim neatly and gently put another mould on the pastry (this will help the pastry hold its shape). Put the moulds on a baking tray and bake for 5 minutes. Allow the pastry cases to cool in the moulds.

• To make the ganache, heat the cream in a saucepan until almost boiling. Put the chocolate in a bowl and pour over the scalded cream, stirring until the chocolate has melted. Add the butter and mix until well incorporated. Set aside to cool.

• To assemble, remove the cooled pastry cases from the moulds. Spoon the ganache into a piping bag with a small star nozzle and pipe rosettes into the pastry cases. Decorate each petit four with the raspberries and serve.

Note: You can substitute red currants for raspberries. The ganache will keep for a week with refrigeration. The pastry cases will keep for a week in an airtight container.

Makes 20

Almond Macaroons
Chocolate Macaroons

125 g almond meal

250 g icing sugar

2 tablespoons cocoa
  (optional)

2 egg whites

2 teaspoons castor sugar

• Sift the almond meal and icing sugar into a bowl (add the cocoa if making Chocolate Macaroons). In another bowl, whisk the egg whites until stiff peaks form and add the castor sugar. Whisk for a further minute to make a meringue. Fold the sifted ingredients into the meringue and transfer to a piping bag with a small round nozzle. Pipe 3 mm disks onto trays lined with baking paper. Allow to dry for 1 hour.

• Preheat the oven to 170°C. Bake for about 10 minutes.

• Remove the trays from the oven and pour cold water under the baking paper to release the macaroons. Dust the almond macaroons lightly with icing sugar (if making Chocolate Macaroons dust with cocoa powder) and serve.

Makes 15

Lemon Tartlettes

150 g Sablé Pastry

(see page 123)

1 lemon

150 g castor sugar

100 g unsalted butter

3 eggs

125 ml water

125 g sugar

• Preheat the oven to 180°C.

• Roll out the pastry on a lightly floured surface to 3 mm thickness. Using a pastry cutter or knife, cut 20 rounds slightly larger than the petit four moulds (25 mm–30 mm). Lightly smear the moulds with butter and line with pastry. Trim neatly and gently place another mould on the pastry (this will help the pastry hold its shape). Put the moulds on a tray and bake for 5 minutes. Allow the pastry cases to cool in the moulds.

• To make lemon curd, squeeze the lemon to obtain 4 tablespoons juice (reserve shells for later use). In a double boiler, combine the lemon juice, castor sugar, butter and eggs and cook, stirring continuously over a gentle heat, until the mixture coats the back of a spoon.

• Remove the rind from the lemon and cut into julienne (or use a zester). Put the zest, water and sugar into a saucepan and bring it to the boil. Gently simmer for about 2 minutes. Remove from the heat and cool in the pan.

• Remove the cooled pastry cases from the moulds. Spoon the curd into a piping bag with a small star nozzle and pipe rosettes into the pastry shells. Garnish with a piece of lemon zest and serve.

Makes 20

Coconut Tuiles

2 **eggs**

125 g **icing sugar**

125 g **shredded coconut**

15 g **unsalted butter,**
    melted

100 g **chocolate (optional)**

• Preheat the oven to 170°C.

• Whisk the eggs and icing sugar in a bowl until well mixed. Using a spatula, fold the coconut through the mixture, then the butter.

• Line a tray with baking paper and spoon on half a teaspoon of mixture. Spread the mixture into a thin round and repeat this process until all the mixture has been used.

• Bake for 5 minutes or until lightly golden.

• Using a spatula, carefully remove a warm tuile from the baking paper. Mould the tuile around a rolling pin, then remove and allow to cool on a wire rack. Repeat this process with the remaining biscuits.

• If desired, melt the chocolate and dip half of each tuile into it. Allow to set on a wire rack.

Makes 20

Hot Cross Buns

280 g bakers' flour

pinch of salt

1 teaspoon powdered milk

1 teaspoon cinnamon

1 teaspoon mixed spice

2 tablespoons sugar

12 g (1 sachet) dry yeast

1 egg

150 ml water

125 g sultanas

60 g currants

1 dessertspoon
  mixed peel

CROSS MIXTURE

125 g plain flour

75 ml water

10 ml vegetable oil

SUGAR SYRUP

75 ml water

75 g sugar

25 ml brandy

• Sift the dry ingredients, except the yeast, into a mixing bowl with a dough hook. Add the yeast, egg and water and mix for 10 minutes. Add in the fruit and peel, and rest the dough for 1 hour.

• Knock back the dough by pushing your fist into it. Divide into small rolls (about 60 g each) and arrange on a tray lined with baking paper. Allow the dough to prove, covered with a tea towel, for 1 hour.

• Preheat the oven to 220°C.

• Make the Cross Mixture by mixing the ingredients at high speed with a balloon whisk for 2 minutes. Make a cross on each bun and bake for 25 minutes.

• For the Sugar Syrup bring all the ingredients to the boil. Paint the hot buns with the syrup and allow to cool on a wire rack.

Makes 12

Just as food **sustains** the individual, festivals sustain the culture. Festivals, then can be seen as the food of culture.

Anthony Coronas

Tools of the trade: a piping bag and a pastry brush

Plum Pudding

3 eggs

200 g brown sugar

125 g plain flour

125 g breadcrumbs

pinch of cinnamon

1/2 teaspoon mixed spice

pinch of nutmeg

FRUIT MIX

1/2 orange

1/2 lemon

250 ml guinness

75 ml brandy

pinch of salt

275 g raisins

185 g sultanas

185 g currants

150 g almonds, chopped

75 g mixed peel

75 g glacé cherries

200 g suet, grated

1/2 apple, peeled
  and grated

1/2 carrot, peeled
  and grated

• To make the Fruit Mix, grate and juice the orange and lemon and add to a large bowl with the remaining ingredients. Stir the mixture thoroughly and allow to macerate for a minimum of 6 weeks, turning it each week.

• To make the pudding, cream the eggs and sugar in a large bowl and fold in the flour, breadcrumbs, spices and macerated fruit and mix well. Divide the mixture between two (500 g–700 g) pudding basins. Place a round of greaseproof paper over the top of each pudding and press down firmly to make them watertight (steamproof).

• Preheat the oven to 180°C.

• Tightly wrap the pudding basins with muslin cloth and secure with string under the rim of each bowl. Put the puddings in roasting trays ➤

and fill the trays with
enough water to come
halfway up the sides of the
basins. Cover the trays with
foil, making a hole in the
centre to allow steam to
escape. Bake for 8 hours,
checking regularly that the
water level remains halfway
up the puddings. If the water
level drops, top up as
required.

• After baking remove
puddings from the roasting
trays and cool for 24 hours.

• To reheat the pudding,
place the pudding in a pot
with water halfway up the
sides. Bring to the boil and
then simmer for 30 minutes.
To microwave, reheat on
high for 8 minutes.
Serve with Brandy Sauce
(see page 120).

Makes 2

the
bas

the basics

ics

Custard

250 ml cream

250 ml milk

3 egg yolks

50 g castor sugar

• Put the cream and milk in a saucepan and heat until almost boiling. Remove from the heat.

• In another bowl, mix the yolks and sugar well. Add three-quarters of the milk and cream to the yolks and sugar and mix.

• Return the mixture to the saucepan and cook over a gentle heat, stirring, until the mixture coats the back of a spoon. Do not boil or the yolks will curdle.

• Serve with cakes.

BRANDY SAUCE

Stir 3 tablespoons brandy through the cooled Custard and serve with Plum Pudding (see page 115).

RASPBERRY SAUCE

Stir 3 tablespoons raspberry liqueur through the cooled Custard and serve with Heart-shaped Raspberry Charlotte (see page 100).

PEACH SAUCE

Stir 3 tablespoons peach tree liqueur through the cooled Custard and serve with Peach Charlotte (see page 71).

Makes 600 ml

Raspberry Mousse

160 g fresh raspberries

2¹/₂ tablespoons sugar

3 level teaspoons
  powdered gelatine

160 ml cream

• Purée the raspberries in a blender or food processor, and then pass the purée through a fine sieve. Discard the contents of the sieve.

• In a saucepan, cook the raspberry purée and sugar on a gentle heat until the sugar has dissolved.

• Dissolve the gelatine in a little of the raspberry purée and then stir it into the rest. Suspend the saucepan over a bowl filled with ice to cool, or refrigerate.

• When the raspberry purée has cooled, whip the cream softly and fold into the purée. Refrigerate until required.

Note: This mousse is used in the Heart-shaped Raspberry Charlotte (see page 100) and is a favourite component of petits fours.

Makes 1 cup

Leaven Pastry

12 g (1 sachet) dry yeast

500 g bakers' flour

100 ml water

200 ml milk

2 tablespoons sugar

1 dessertspoon salt

300 g unsalted butter,

   not too firm or soft

• Mix the yeast and 50 g of the flour together in a bowl, then add the water. Whisk and put aside in a warm place to prove for 15 minutes or until doubled in size.

• In an electric mixer put the milk into the bowl and then add the sugar, salt and remaining flour and mix until the dough just comes together.

This pastry is suitable for Croissants (page 80), Pain au Chocolat (page 86) and escargots.

• Remove the dough and roll into a rectangle 40 cm x 76 cm and about 8 mm thick. Refrigerate (this stops it proving) for 1½ hours.

• Put the dough on a lightly floured surface with the long edge towards you. Put the butter at one end of the dough and spread it over that half. Fold the other half of dough over the butter and pinch the sides of the dough around the butter. Turn the dough one quarter of a turn clockwise so that the seams now face you. Roll out the dough and butter parallel to you to the same thickness (8 mm), making sure that the ends keep square. Fold the dough three-quarters down its own length, right side to left, then place the remaining dough on the left over the dough previously folded. You should have a square shape

Sablé Pastry

of three layers. Turn the dough one quarter of a turn clockwise towards you; the end of the top layer should be facing you. Repeat the above procedure. Refrigerate the dough for 1 hour, then repeat the above procedure once more. Refrigerate the dough until firm enough for rolling out and cutting into croissants.

Note: The pastry and butter should be at the same temperature and have the same degree of firmness.

Makes 1.2 kg

610 g flour
250 g icing sugar
pinch of salt
500 g unsalted butter, softened
5 egg yolks

• Using an electric mixer with a paddle, mix the dry ingredients and add the butter in pieces, then slowly add the egg yolks. When the pastry comes together, remove from the bowl.
• Divide the pastry into manageable amounts. Cover with plastic wrap and chill to a workable temperature.

Note: This pastry can be frozen.

Makes 1.5 kg

Puff Pastry

500 g flour

200 ml cold water

1 teaspoon salt

2 tablespoons vinegar

500 g butter, firm but not soft

• Place the flour on the table. Make a well in the centre and add the water, salt and vinegar. Work gently to form a firm paste.

• Knead the dough for 2 minutes, then wrap it in plastic and refrigerate for 2–3 hours.

• Roll out the chilled dough from each corner to an 18 cm square to form an 'envelope' in the middle. Place the butter in the centre and fold over the dough to make a parcel.

• With a rolling pin, make quick, firm rolls away from you. The dough should be pliable but not soft.

• Roll out the dough to a 70 cm x 40 cm rectangle. Fold into thirds. You should now have 3 layers.

• Wrap the dough in plastic and return to the refrigerator for 30 minutes.

• Turn the chilled dough a quarter of a turn on the work bench and repeat the rolling process. This time the seams should be to your left. (The seams should be on your left every alternate time you work the dough.) With each turn the pastry becomes a little thinner.

• Do a total of 6 turns, refrigerating the dough for 30 minutes after each turn. The pastry should be even in colour and not streaky. Allow the pastry to stand refrigerated for at least an hour before use.

Makes 1.2 kg

Sheet Sponge

8 eggs, separated

185 g sugar

1 teaspoon vanilla

185 g plain flour

• Preheat the oven to 220°C.

• Whisk the egg whites until peaks form. Slowly add the sugar, then the yolks and vanilla and turn off the mixer immediately. Fold in the flour by hand.

• Using a plain 1 cm nozzle, pipe the mixture to make 2 rectangles 60 cm x 40 cm on trays lined with baking paper. Bake for 7–10 minutes or until the sponge starts to brown. Be careful not to overcook or the sponge will become dry and hard.

• Turn the sponge out to cool.

Makes one 50 cm x 30 cm sheet

HEART-SHAPED

RASPBERRY

CHARLOTTE

• To make a two-toned sponge for the Raspberry Charlotte (see page 100), divide the mixture in two. Carefully mix red food dye through one lot of mixture to make it a deep raspberry colour.

• Using two separate piping bags with plain 1 cm nozzles, pipe the mixture diagonally onto trays lined with baking paper, alternating colours as you go.

• Bake as for the Sheet Sponge.

Génoise Sponge

8 eggs

250 g sugar

250 g plain flour, sifted

50 g unsalted butter,

   melted

• Preheat the oven to 220°C.

• Put the eggs and sugar into a stainless steel bowl and whisk over another bowl filled with hot water until the mixture is light and fluffy (about 5 minutes). Transfer the mixture to an electric mixer and beat until it is cool and falls back on itself in a steady stream when the whisk is lifted from the bowl (about 10 minutes).

• Fold the sifted flour through the mixture very gently, followed by the butter.

• Butter and flour two 22 cm cake rings and divide the mixture between them. Bake for 30 minutes.

• Invert the tins on a wire rack to cool (this will give each sponge a flat top).

Makes 2

Almond Macaroons 106

Baguettes 26
Biscotti Garibaldi 93

Carrot Cake 58
Cheese Sticks 83
Chocolate Macaroons 106
Chocolate and Raspberry
 Tartlettes 105
Coconut Tuiles 109
Concorde 61
Croissants 80
Custard 120

Double-baked
 Chocolate Cake 56
Doughnuts 85

Flat Olive Bread 29
Flourless Chocolate
 Muffins 66

Génoise Sponge 126
Goat's Cheese Tarts 42
Gougère 91

Heart-shaped Raspberry
 Charlotte 100
Hot Cross Buns 110

Lamingtons 54
Leaven Pastry 122
Lemon Tartlettes 107

Mr Roux's Lemon Tart 41

Orange and Poppyseed
 Cake 68

Pain au Chocolat 86
Passionfruit Tart 46
Peach Charlotte 71
Plum Pudding 115
Puff Pastry 124

Raspberry Mousse 121

Sablé Pastry 123
San Francisco Sour
 Dough 18
Savoury Brioches 88
Seasonal Fruitella
 Tart 38
Sheet Sponge 125
Smoked Salmon
 Quiche 36
Sour Rye Bread 22

Vanilla Slice 96

Walnut and Raisin
 Sticks 20

There is no **love**

sincerer than the

love of food.

George Bernard Shaw